Good Night
BOTSWANA

TALES FROM AN EXPEDITION LEADER

Good Night
BOTSWANA

TALES FROM AN EXPEDITION LEADER

RICHARD AVILINO

Photos by Richard Avilino and Gen Guanci
Managing Editor, Gen Guanci
Edited by Katie Cressman
Book design by JamesMonroeDesign.com

ISBN 13: 979-8-9919149-2-5

Library of Congress Control Number: 2025930281

Printed in the United States of America
First Printing: 2025
29   28   27   26   25   5   4   3   2   1

For permission and ordering information, contact: bda15@aol.com

CREATIVE
HEALTH CARE
MANAGEMENT

Creative Health Care Management
8500 Normandale Lake Blvd, Ste 350
Minneapolis, MN 55437 USA

To my grandparents: Selawe and Namasoko; my parents: Sekeseke and Gaebutswe; my uncle: Boitshoko, and my brother: Robert, who planted the seeds of knowledge in my mind and nurtured them.

To my wife: Kay, who has been my most profound inspiration and support of my passion.

To my children: Tshenolo, Rafiwa, and Thea, who continue to inspire me to tell stories that matter.

To Gen: my friend and mentor, who saw in me what I failed to see in myself. Without her support and encouragement this book would not be a reality.

To my expedition guests: who breathe life into these pages.

To Botswana, and all the beauty she has to offer, my source of never-ending inspiration.

CONTENTS

1

THE JOURNEY OF LIFE

I am Richard Avilino, born and raised in Maun, Botswana. Maun, located on the southern aspect of the Okavango Delta, serves as Botswana's principal tourism destination. I was raised by my Grandmother and Grandfather, who were known for their farming expertise. My Grandfather had two large fields divided by the twenty-five mile long road that ran from Maun to Sharobe Village. One of his fields was along the Thamalakane River, and the other was near dry land. During the rainy season, which ran from November through March, my cousins and I worked in our Grandfather's fields. We woke up before the sun rose each morning to have our Grandfather's Donkeys plowing before heading to school. My Grandfather also had a large herd of cattle that I helped care for. This was one of my favorite responsibilities, as I loved being with the animals.

Looking back, I realize life was so easy-going in those years. One experience in particular sticks in my mind. One day, I woke up even earlier than usual to milk the Cows before leaving for school. As I was walking to their pen, I came upon a large animal standing at the entrance to the enclosure. Thinking it was just an Oxen that had escaped, I continued my approach. As I confidently marched, as only a young boy can do, towards the enclosure, I realized it was not an Oxen but some beast unknown to me. It turned and looked directly at me! Surprised and a bit frightened, I ran back to the house as fast as my young legs could take me and woke my Grandfather. He quickly accompanied me back to the enclosure to help identify my foreign beast. His deep, rumbling laugh sounded throughout the area as soon as we arrived. He asked me, "Do you not know what that massive animal is?" I replied by shaking my head no. He told me it was a Tshukudu (Setswana name for Rhinoceros).

As the sun continued to rise and daylight blanketed the area, the Rhinoceros slowly continued grazing while moving away from the enclosure. He was no threat to my Grandfather's animals. I'll never forget my first Rhinoceros sighting; that memory is forever etched in my mind!

When I reached 17, I moved from my grandparent's farm to live with my Dad and Mum. My parents lived in a small village called Kgapamadi, where I previously visited them during school holidays. My Dad had a thriving vegetable garden along the Thamalakane River, Maun. The harvest from his garden was used to supply most of the game and tourist lodges in Maun. In addition, because his vegetables were known to be of high-quality, local people would seek him out when they wished to buy produce in bulk.

My Uncle also inspired me growing up, especially when I was living with my Grandfather and Grandmother. He worked in tourism in the Okavango Delta at a camp called Makutsomo a Bokhutho along the Santantadibe River. The Okavango Delta, spanning 2,316 to 5,791 square miles in northwest Botswana, consists of permanent swamps and seasonally flooded areas. It is also a natural wonder of the world and an UNESCO World Heritage Site. The Delta is home to vast numbers of animals and birds, including Elephants, Lions, Impala, Red Lechwe, African Fish Eagles, Pell's Fishing Owls, Yellow-Billed Storks, and a variety of Bee-eaters.

My first visit to my Uncle's camp was during one of my school holidays. It was also my first experience spending multiple nights sleeping in a small tent. The first night, I could not sleep because of the various sounds of nature bombarding me from all directions. Elephants munching on berries from the Jackalberry tree, Hyenas making their whooping calls back and forth to each other, and, never to be forgotten, the roar of a Lion that caused my tent to tremble through my tent. Indeed, it was a terrifying night for me as a young boy alone in his tent. Still, I yearned for more.

After completing my primary level education, I continued to senior secondary school. My older Brother worked in the Okavango Delta at "Delta Camp" during this time. "Delta Camp" was one of the original safari camps in the Moremi Game Reserve. He invited me to visit him on my school holiday. I flew to Delta Camp in a tiny, 6-passenger Cessna 206, and seeing the Delta from the plane's window was awe-inspiring. Water and green were everywhere my eyes looked. Small round islands, made from termite mounds and populated with trees and brush, dotted the landscape. I could even see maternal herds of Elephants containing all ages and sizes.

During my time with my Brother, he took me out on activities like Mokoro rides. A Mokoro, the primary transportation method in the Okavango Delta, is a canoe-type vessel made from a hollowed-out Hardwood Tree. Individuals using long wooden poles silently propel the Mokoro through the water. Stealthy moving through the water while listening only to the sounds of nature was eye-opening for me. Nothing can compare with the sound of Red Lechwe running through the water or the screeching call of an African Fish Eagle. My time with my Brother made my love and passion for African animals and all nature has to offer forever entrenched in my heart. When I think back, I am blessed to have so many members of my family involved in my early nature experiences, which, in turn, fueled my true calling as an adult.

Dumela—Hello

2

CLIMBING THE CAREER LADDER

In my local language, Setswana, we say "setlhare ga se pal-amelwe ko dikaleng," meaning "a tree can't be climbed from the branches." In other words, everything must start at the bottom before getting to the top. Like most teens, I was unsure what I wanted to do in my life. During those young years, my brother gave me some sage advice and recommended I venture into tourism. Heeding his advice, I began in safari tourism as a chef and soon progressed to camp manager at a camp in the Okavango Delta. The camp was run by a company called "Crocodile Camp Safaris" out of Maun. The company's owner, a kind and observant man, saw something beyond a camp manager in me. He said he liked my demeanor, ability to connect with the guests, and passion for nature. With his support and encouragement, I was introduced to the camp's boating excursions, which the guides took the guests on. These boating adventures further solidified my love for being out in the wild. Whenever I traveled with experienced guides, I turned into a sponge! I watched, listened to, and learned from all they did and shared with the groups. After boating and away from the tourists, I asked so many questions that I am sure the guides were tired of me. Every day spent in the wild, my knowledge and confidence grew.

As my experiences accumulated with the various guides, I realized that being out in the wild and being able to share my passion with others was exactly what I wanted to do! With my new-found knowledge and confidence, I decided to enroll in the professional guiding course offered at the Botswana Wildlife Training Institute in Maun. The Institute operates under the Botswana Department of Wildlife & National Parks and the Botswana Ministry of Environment, Wildlife, and Tourism. Completing the program ensured my eligibility to sit for my professional guide examination. Although worth it, to say this was a challenging exam is an understatement. It was a two-day examination that included both theory and practice; wildlife and birds. Imagine having to identify pictures of birds and wild-life that flashed on a screen for two or three seconds. The visual on the screen was so quick that if I blinked, I would miss it. I had 1 try per slide; either I got it or I didn't. My long hours of hard studying paid off. I passed my examination and received my Professional Guide license.

Just because I had my license didn't mean I was ready to lead my own trips. I continued to refine my knowledge and expertise by traveling with experienced field guides who were leading mobile safaris. A mobile safari is when a group travels to multiple locations, and the overnight camp is erected specifically for that group. The next day, the camp is dismantled and moved with the group to the following location. Mobile camps are a more rustic, adventurous experience, complete with small tents and water bucket showers.

After many trips shadowing the experienced field guides, the time finally arrived for me to independently lead my first trip. I was filled with excitement and trepidation. I was on my own with the full responsibility of leading nine guests through the pristine areas of Botswana for fourteen days. The trip, which I felt good about, ended on the Zambian side of the stunning Victoria Falls, one of the Seven Natural Wonders of the World. Victoria Falls is referred to by Zambian locals as Mosi-oa-Tunya, or the smoke that thunders. The name reflects the mist rising from thousands of gallons of water flowing from the Zambezi River over the Falls, which produces a large amount of mist that looks like smoke and makes a roaring sound as it tumbles into the gorge.

As is customary at the end of every trip, the guests are asked to evaluate their experience. I handed over evaluations to the guests so they could share their feedback and assessments of their trip, and of course, me. I was nervous. Did they like my leadership style and knowledge? Did I meet their needs? What might they say I could improve on? Later that evening, I reviewed their feedback. I received high marks from every guest! With one successful trip under my belt, I continued growing in confidence to ensure an extraordinary guest experience every time.

The news of my evaluation feedback from my trips traveled and eventually reached the desk of the Chief Executive Officer at Crocodile Camp Safaris. Soon, I was called into his office, where he shared that he was extremely pleased with my work and the feedback I was receiving. In fact, he said that he was so pleased that he wanted to send me to Germany. Confused, I asked him why. His response? "To learn to speak German, of course!" This made sense to me since most of the clients traveling with us were from Germany, and their experience could only be enhanced by having a German-speaking guide. A few short months later, my Visa application was completed, and my travel was arranged.

Imagine being thirty years old and leaving your homeland to go to a foreign country to learn a new language! Luckily, I quickly picked up the language and only spent six months in Düsseldorf learning German. While I enjoyed my time in Germany, I was glad to return to Botswana after the time away. Upon return, I was responsible for leading German and Swiss departures until the company closed in 2004.

The closure of Crocodile Camp Safaris did not stop me from pursuing my passion. In 2005, I joined Wilderness Travel, leading migration route trips. Most people are familiar with the Great Migration in Tanzania, yet few know that Botswana has the second-largest migration of Wildebeest, Buffalo, and Zebras. The migration occurs seasonally as the animals move, searching for the best grazing land.

Through my experience at Wilderness Travel, I became familiar with the United States-based company Natural Habitat Adventures. The company's eco-travel and conservation efforts intrigued me, and the fact they had been a World Wildlife Fund partner since 2003 only added to my admiration. In 2006, I interviewed with NatHab for a position as an Expedition Leader. I liked what I heard and saw about NatHab, and they liked what they saw and heard about me. Once they offered me a position, I eagerly accepted. I was now an employee of NatHab, the most respected and known company in the eco and conservation travel field.

My first trips with Natural Habitat Adventures were their Botswana Explorer trips. These "Adventure Camps" consisted of accommodations in small dome tents, latrine toilets, and bush showers (a 5-gallon bucket of water that hung at the back of the tents). I loved these trips as we were immersed in nature and covered more distance from one camp to the other. I am not convinced all my guests would agree with my love, as long days in a safari vehicle traversing dirt roads are not the most comfortable travel experiences. Yet, despite the long days and arriving at our next camp after sunset, the experience that guests had on each trip was hard to beat. Our travels from camp to camp were really game drives. The abundance of wildlife and birds sighted along the way was top-notch. We always arrived at camp tired yet pleased with what the day had brought.

Tsamaya sentle—Go well

3

EXPECTATIONS VARY

Being a guide for different nationalities is always a fascinating, educational, and eye-opening experience. Several years ago, I had a twelve-day trip with seven Eastern European guests. They were doing an "Adventure Camp" trip where their accommodations would be far from luxurious, in the small dome tents with only bucket showers to wash with. In addition, at that time, there was no internet access in the Adventure Camps. I met my guests in Kasane as they arrived from their time spent at Victoria Falls. The plan upon arrival was to proceed to the Chobe River to enjoy a sightseeing boat cruise.

As scheduled, the bus arrived, and passengers gradually disembarked. The first thing that surprised me was the way my guests were dressed. The females wore white dresses and high heels, which were beautiful outfits, but not what I would describe as safari-friendly or practical attire. Regardless of their dress, we proceeded to our cruise as planned. Only two of the seven guests were interested in the scenery and wildlife. The interested pair asked plenty of questions and took lots of pictures while the remaining five had their heads down as they concentrated on their phones.

After the relaxing boat cruise, we faced the long dirt road transfer from Kasane to the Linyanti Adventure Camp. As we transferred to our vehicle, one guest asked if any wine was onboard. Our cooler bag contained water and a variety of soft drinks, but alas, there was no wine. However, I offered to take them to a store where we could pick up some wine, and they eagerly accepted!

Partway through our journey from Kasane to Linyanti, the guests finished the wine and asked where to get more. Knowing there was only Kachikao ahead, the final small village we would pass through on our trip, I promised to stop there and check. Finding any wine in a small African village is a challenge, never mind fine wine, so the only wine available was from an inexpensive brand. However, my guests did not seem to mind, as they bought several bottles. Once again supplied with wine, we continued on our trek to Linyanti. If you have ever ridden in a safari vehicle on African roads, you know that the word "roads" is relative. African bush roads are dirt or sand tracks peppered with ruts and bumps. These tracks do not offer the smooth ride guests are familiar with from back home. In the middle of our journey, one lady urgently said, "Stop!" and quickly jumped out of the vehicle to empty the contents of her stomach. Lesson learned: cheap wine and African roads do not go well together.

We arrived at our camp late in the evening, and with no other mishaps, and after dinner, the guests settled into their tents. The following morning, we arose early for breakfast and then set out on our planned game drive, where we saw one young male Lion. Unfortunately, he was skittish and kept relatively out of sight behind a bush. Guests on other trips would have been disappointed by this limited sighting, yet it did not bother this group as they were more interested in what was on their iPads.

Back at camp, the guests had free time to do whatever they wished. A while later, a few guests approached me to inquire if it would be possible to get a flight to Sun City, a high-end resort northwest of Johannesburg, South Africa. They shared that their request was driven by the camp accommodation not meeting their standards. In addition, the fact that there was no internet was something they could not move past. I organized for all but two guests to fly out the next morning. The two remaining guests were the two who had shown interest in the wildlife while we were on our river cruise the day before. One shared with me that his travel companions' behavior embarrassed him. He explained that before the trip, he had shared with them what to expect on our journey. This proves that safari life is not for everyone.

Sometimes, other guide groups and guests would share our camps. I remember one example that occurred while I was leading a group in the Kalahari Desert. The Kalahari Desert, a flat 350,000-acre area, receives five to ten inches of rainfall annually. Because of this rainfall, it is disqualified from being a true desert. Despite the rain that quickly passes through the deep sand, the landscape remains barren, with a view many describe as what the moon's surface looks like. When we arrived at camp for our three-night stay, we noticed several other guests, with their guides, were also staying there. We soon discovered that the guests included a European couple who had booked a private game drive.

An important note to this story is that our arrival (in December) coincided with the beginning of the area's rainy season, which brings many ground-dwelling bugs out into the open. Millipedes were abundant. While harmless, Millipedes are bizarre-looking creatures with dozens of legs that move synchronously.

Walking to the main area for breakfast one morning, I noticed a camp guide carrying a female guest on his back.

Perplexed, I stopped and watched as they headed for the main area of the camp. I had no idea what was going on. Once at the main area, the female guest climbed down from the guide's back, settled into a chair, and proceeded to enjoy breakfast with her companion and the guide who carried her. Fascinated by this scene, I kept my eyes open to see if I could figure out what was going on. Once breakfast was done, the female guest and her companion prepared for their private game drive. In this case, the preparation consisted of her settling, once again, on the back of her guide. Upon her arrival at the main area, she climbed off the guide's back and settled in when she arrived at the safari vehicle.

I noticed this strange practice reoccurred when they returned from their game drive and headed back to their tent. Curiosity was getting the better of me, so I asked the guide, "Why are you carrying your guest on your back?" Nonchalantly, he replied, "Millipedes frighten my guest." That prompted my next question, "How long is the couple's stay at the camp?" "Six nights," he said. I shook my head and told him good luck! I found out later that this was not the first time this guest had been carried by a guide, as they were frequent travelers to Botswana and the area. Not only do safari guides provide thrilling wildlife experiences, but they also do whatever it takes to ensure guests are happy—no matter how strange the request!

Boroko—Good night

4

ADVENTURE CAMPS

Adventure camps have always been my favorite trip destination because they leave familiar amenities, such as electricity and plumbing, behind and give one a sense of what it might have been like for early African travelers. One of these camps was located in the Linyanti Concession, which is approximately 30,000 acres spread in the north east region of Botswana, between Chobe and the Okavango Delta. The Concession is untouched, unspoiled wilderness and a haven for the wildlife seen throughout Botswana.

There is one especially notable afternoon drive here that I always remember fondly. As we were driving west along the Linyanti fault line, I spotted a male Leopard lounging in the shade at the base of a tree. Upon further scanning of the area, I noticed a kill tucked securely in the fork of that tree's branches. I wanted my guests to have a good view of this scene, so I parked the vehicle to give them a view of both the Leopard and its kill. We all spent the next forty-five minutes observing the scene while I shared some facts about what we were viewing.

Eventually, with the guests satisfied and having taken the photos they wanted, I slowly started to pull away from the site. As I did this, one of my guests in the very back of the vehicle asked several questions. She began, "Richard, why was there an Impala up in the tree branches?" I was intrigued by her question, yet I thought perhaps she had not heard my previous elaborations since she sat in the vehicle row furthest from me. I replied that it was the Leopard's he carried up and stored in the tree to prevent other predators, such as Lions and Hyenas, from stealing it. Her next question perplexed both the guests and me. "When do you think the Leopard will return to claim its kill?" she asked. While motioning in the tree's direction, I replied that the Leopard was lying in the shade of the tree directly below the kill. Confused, she said she didn't see a Leopard under the tree. Needless to say, this took me and the guests by surprise. Variations of "Are you serious" or "Are you joking?" resonated through our vehicle. Equally confused by these comments, she said, "I'm serious."

Turning the vehicle around, I returned to the area and pulled close, pointing out the majestic male Leopard lying under the tree. It took her a while, but finally, she saw him! I listened to the other guests ask her what she had been looking at before while sitting there. She replied, "I was looking at the kill up in the tree."

At this point, it was clear that she must not have heard me when I pointed out the Leopard when we first pulled up to the tree. However, once the vehicle stopped and the additional noises had faded, she could hear me and listened closely as I pointed out the kill securely tucked in the tree. She said she was so excited to see the kill in the tree that she missed everything else I had shared.

The entire group shook their heads as they could not fathom anyone being so mesmerized by an Impala kill in a tree that they would sit for forty-five minutes looking at it while missing the Leopard lying not more than a few yards away from us. The more I thought about it, the more I respected

and understood her fascination with seeing an Impala tucked in the tree. The Leopard's ability to climb, often vertical trees, combined with the ability to do so while carrying their kill, is unique in the animal kingdom. The strength and agility of a Leopard to get the kill safely up a tree and then tucked securely in place is awe-inspiring. We recalled this experience several times throughout the remainder of the trip. The entire group chuckled every time and said, "This is one for the books"!

kwa ntle mo sekgweng—out in the bush

5

HERE KITTY, KITTY

The Okavango Delta's vastness and beauty make it one of my favorite places. Wild animals in the area range from Hippopotamuses to Elephants, Otters, and even Lions who are not concerned about swimming from island to island. One time, I was enjoying camping out on a termite-mound-created island with only one guest.

The guest and I decided to go on a game drive one morning. Delta game drives typically occur on the water since it is fed by a vast network of water channels that flood often beginning in April, after the Botswana wet season. This flooding lasts many months, making water travel the easiest method. During this time, travel is conducted via a Mokoro (the dugout canoe I mentioned earlier) while being propelled by a poler. However, we decided our "drive" would be a land-based walking event on that particular day. After breakfast, the poler, my guest, and I set off on walking and were enjoying the sights,

sounds, and smells along the way. After more than an hour of walking, we decided to take a break under a beautiful Jackalberry Tree. As always, I scanned the area to ensure we were safe. In the distance, I spotted a pride of Lions walking across the island. I did not have a complete view, as the grass was a bit high. Wanting a better view and knowing that elevation would help, I asked my guest and poler to walk to a mound between us and the distant Lions.

At the same time, the Lions also changed their direction and headed to the same mound as us, but because the grass was high, I had yet to notice their movements. We were about 50 yards away from our new lookout spot when I spotted two rounded, tawny ears on the other side of the mound. I quickly told the poler and guest to stand still. Asking why, I shared that the Lions had arrived at the same mound. Suddenly, multiple sets of ears perked up from the grass. As I tried to evaluate the scene, a young male Lion rose from behind the mound while the rest of his family remained lying down. Remembering the number one bush rule, I told the others that whatever you do, don't run.

Upon spotting us, the young male Lion started to growl. Because my group's safety is always my top priority, I positioned myself in front and kept checking on the Lion, the rest of the pride, the guest, and the polar. After scanning the area again, I was convinced the situation only involved the single Lion. I told the group to slowly take a step backward without turning around. With every step we took away from the pride, the young Lion's growling became louder, and his posture grew more aggressive. Suddenly, he charged at us in full force while growling so intensely that I could feel the ground shake.

I shouted to the poler and guest to freeze, which, thankfully, they instantly did.

At the time of the Lion's charge, I had nothing in my hands- no weapon to ward off the attacking Lion. Looking at my hands then, I found myself holding a stick, and I had no idea when, where, or how I got it. I remembered learning in my Expedition certificate training that if I roared back at the Lion while making myself as large as possible, this might stop the Lion's forward movement. Deciding I had no other options, I tried this. Confused, the Lion stopped and just stared back at me. He probably held that stare for about a minute, yet it felt like two hours. The rest of the pride had no interest in what the young male was up to, and soon, they stood up and ambled away. Realizing his pride was moving on, the male Lion turned and followed them.

Silently, our group walked back to our camping ground. Once back at our camp, the poler came to me and told me he would not spend another night in the area. I asked him why, and he shared that he was going to have nightmares every night about what happened to us on our walk. I tried to convince him it would be okay since we only had one more night on the island before returning to the main camp. Not pleased with my response, he walked away with tears running down his cheeks, leaving me to sit under a tree alone.

Later that afternoon, another group arrived in our area and decided to camp next to us. I noticed the group had two polers, so I approached their leader and asked if they would allow the poler carrying the equipment to join my group so that I could release my poler. After some negotiations, it worked out, and my poler returned to the camp with his Mokoro. Once there, he arranged for another poler and Mokoro to come and transport us back to the camp the following day. Upon returning to camp, I checked on him. He told me that the walking safari we had been on was his first and last because it was his first time encountering Lions. I guess you can say not everyone is a lover of cats!

Pudi matseba—Stay alert

6

INSPIRED

As an Expedition Leader for a Colorado-based travel company, most of my guests are from various US States. I believe that I am fortunate to represent this travel company, Natural Habitat Adventures (NatHab), in Botswana, Zimbabwe, and Zambia. I get to meet so many people every year, and occasionally, I will meet a guest that I really click with. Someone as passionate about nature as I am. Someone with a thirst to learn and a willingness to fully engage in the experience. Someone who can take my sense of humor and give it back to me. One such guest was an American traveler named Gen. She traveled to Africa on her own, which immediately told me there was something special about her.

We first met in August of 2023 on a Secluded Botswana Safari. From day one, she was mesmerized by the sights and sounds and engaged me by asking many questions. It was clear she had prepared herself for the trip as she knew many details about the animals we saw. To say Gen loved her first safari experience is an understatement. Even before she left, she was thinking about returning. At the end of the trip, Gen asked me if I had any recommendations for another safari in Botswana, so I recommended NatHab's "Kalahari, the Delta, and Beyond" trip. She wondered what would be different on that trip from the one she was currently on. I shared that this safari occurs during Botswana's green (or rainy) season; therefore, she would experience the lush foliage of the area, teaming with migrating animals.

Gen and I stayed in touch after she left, and she told me she booked her return trip shortly after she had gotten home. However, just returning to Botswana was not good enough for her. She had a specific trip requirement: that I be the trip's Expedition Leader. Since my Expedition Leader schedule hadn't been developed yet for that year, NatHab agreed to her request and assigned me as the Leader for that trip's date. Gen returned to Botswana six months later for her Green Season trip.

I typically begin my safaris by asking guests what they wish to see or experience during their time with me. Since Gen had not seen a Cheetah on her first trip, that was number one on her list. Also on her list were Meerkats, which I assured her would happen when we got to the Kalahari since I knew our travels would include visiting a mob of habituated Meerkats. As the trip progressed, I tried my best to fulfill her and the group's experience wish lists. Unfortunately, I could not find a Cheetah for Gen. She did, however, get to visit a family of Meerkats.

At our last dinner on the safari, the guests decided to grade me on their experience. A, A+, beyond an A+, resonated

from all the guests except Gen. She told me that while she would give me an A+ for effort, my overall grade could only be "incomplete." Shocked by her response, everyone asked why. With a twinkle in her eye, she looked at me and said the grade was because I did not find a Cheetah for her. She continued to explain that because of the "incomplete" grade, she would be "forced" to return to Africa again! We all laughed at that, as it was apparent she just wanted an excuse to return.

Gen booked her third safari with plans to return seven months later. She again requested that I be her Expedition Leader, and after some schedule adjustments, I was able to accept and was very happy to do so.

When I asked my group at dinner on the first night of Gen's third return trip what they wished to experience, their requests were fairly general; Elephants, Lions, Leopards, Giraffes, etc. This was not the same for Gen's third trip list since she knew those sightings from her prior visits. Of course, Cheetahs remained on the top of her list, while the remaining items were quite specific and ones that only an experienced safari goer would think of. Not only did she list animals, but she also listed specific activities she wanted to see them doing! A Leopard lying on a tree branch with all their legs hanging down. A baby Elephant twirling its truck as they tried to learn how to use it. The up-close sound of a Lion's roar. And, of course, lots of wildlife babies!

I laughed and shook my head as I listened to the specific list, knowing no one could control nature. You could also see the skepticism on her fellow travelers' faces. However, we would be shocked even more once Gen somehow checked off most of what she had on her list!

Toward the end of our first afternoon game drive, we came across a young Leopard on a tree branch with all four legs hanging down over the branch. I looked at Gen, who smiled while making a check mark sign in the air, indicating she was checking this sighting off her list.

At the next camp, Gen ended up checking off three more items from her list. Finally, she saw a mother Cheetah with four cubs that we observed and followed for a while. Check!

Next were two female Lions with two cubs each. Two of the cubs were about four months old, while the others were only about one month old. Check; another item crossed off Gen's list. It didn't end there, though. We went on to see a Leopard with a three or four-month-old cub and African Wild dogs with puppies in tow. Double check! Guests began to wonder if Gen had a direct communication line to Mother Nature, as her list provided incredible sights for the entire group.

We completed even more sightings from Gen's list at our next campsite. We followed a male Lion as he sauntered down the road, all the while roaring to let other Lions know this was his territory. While not on Gen's list, we encountered a clan of Hyenas that included several three-month-old baby Hyenas. If you have ever seen an adult Hyena, you know they are not considered attractive. This made the utter cuteness of the baby Hyenas unexpected and incredibly appreciated. This was not lost on Gen, who said they ranked as one of her favorite sightings of that trip!

I often share a safari experience story or two with guests during safari dinners. Knowing I have many stories I can share, Gen had a word with me one evening. She said, "Richard, you should write a book with your experience and stories." I agreed with her, yet I had no idea how to do that. How do I get started? Who will edit for me? How will I get it published? Without any prompting, she offered, "I will help!" Gen, an author herself, shared she had the contacts needed to make this book a reality. She told me to just start writing my stories, so after dinner, I went to my tent and did just that. I was surprised to find that the writing flowed easily, and by the end of the night, I had already emailed several pages to Gen, and our dinner idea became a reality.

Later the next day, Gen told me she liked what I wrote, and I was definitely on the right track. "Well done, Richard, well done," she said. That was all the encouragement and motivation I needed. During every bit of free time that I had, I was busy writing. I wrote late into the night, after lunch, and even early in the morning. My writing continued even after Gen returned to the States, and soon, she had so much from me she asked me to pause until she could do the editing and see what we ended up with.

Gen not only encouraged me to write but also came up with the book title and design. I consider Gen to be my mentor, yet more importantly, to be my friend. Never doubt that there are people in this world who open paths for others out of the goodness of their hearts.

Tsala—Friend

7

NIGHT SKY

If you ever spent the night sleeping in the open under the stars, I am sure you can relate to the feeling that comes with being one with nature. I have always loved doing this; looking up and seeing the Milky Way and other constellations of stars while listening to the sound of the nighttime bush is always an awe-inspiring experience.

On one particular trip, we arrived at our campsite later than usual. I always help the guests set up whatever they need for the night. That evening, I was so tired after helping guests pitch their dome tents that I decided not to pitch mine. Instead, I would sleep under the stars. This evening, I decided the top of our vehicle was a comfortable place to set up my "bed" and spend the night. This location ensured I was off the ground, away from the insects and nocturnal creatures.

After dinner, the guests and I relaxed sitting around the bush TV (the firepit). While enjoying some after-dinner drinks, guests shared stories about their home lives, families, and past travel adventures. I, in turn, shared several stories from my life as an Expedition Leader. Eventually, we all retired for the night, as the next day would bring another full schedule of adventure.

Looking forward to spending my night under the stars, I returned to the vehicle, where I eagerly climbed to the roof, settled into my bed, and promptly fell asleep. Around midnight, I was abruptly awakened by seed pods falling from the Acacia Tree where I was parked. Half asleep, I did not comprehend what or how this was happening. Coming to my bearings a bit more, I noticed a large male, also known as a bull, Elephant shaking the tree and causing the seed pods to reign down. The pods bounced around me, some drizzling onto the ground and several remaining where they landed on me. With the massive Elephant hovering so close, I had no escape.

The bull was clearly not concerned there was a human in his presence as he began to eagerly pick seed pods off of where they had landed on me. While grabbing the seeds, he also caught the duvet that I was sleeping under. Realizing it was not food, he quickly threw it to the side. I saw his trunk coming directly toward me for the second time, so I promptly rolled myself to the side of the vehicle's roof to avoid contact. Elephants are powerful, and what might be a simple trunk flick could land a devastating injury to whatever the trunk comes in contact with. Unfortunately, I overshot the edge as I rolled to safety and landed with a large thud on the ground. Startled by my abrupt landing, I screamed. My scream was so loud that it woke the guests, and they rushed out of their tents, shouting,

"Richard, are you okay?" Not wanting to share my embarrass-
ment of throwing myself off the roof of the vehicle, I replied I
was fine and was only dreaming. My scream also startled the
Elephant, and thankfully, he promptly left the area instead of
becoming angry and aggressive. I picked myself off the ground
and brushed off the sand and dirt while deciding what to do
now. Wanting to get a bit more sleep, I opened the vehicle door
and settled in to spend the remainder of the night on one of the
seats, safe from any further interruptions. I never did tell the
guests what really happened that night during my sleep under
the night sky.

Tlala—Hungry

8

ANIMAL LEGENDS

There is something mesmerizing about sitting around the bush TV and sharing experiences, which we do countless times during our trips. It is the perfect after-dinner activity to relax and wind down from the day. This is the time when I dig out my favorite stories and legends to share with my guests. My stories, while entertaining, are also educational.

I particularly enjoy sharing why the Common Waterbuck, a large, impressive Antelope, has a white circle on its rump. Each time I tell this story, the guests listen intently as I take them back 1000 years to when Noah built the ark to save the animals from the heavy floods. Everyone knows the dangers of raging water and flooding, but I am especially careful to emphasize that animals are aware of this danger too. In the story, the various animal species began arriving early so they would be ready to enter the ark when Noah gave them the go-ahead. While waiting, the animals went about their business, including last-minute browsing and taking care of any biological "needs" they might have.

When all the animals were loaded, Noah looked around and noticed the Waterbuck was late to arrive and needed to rush to avoid missing the load onto the ark. Flustered, the Waterbuck entered the ark and began desperately looking for a toilet since he had no time before entering the ark to address this biological need. He rushed to the bathroom and, once finished, emerged feeling much better. He just could not understand why the other animals were laughing at him. One of the other animals eventually spoke up and told him that they think the toilet he sat on was freshly painted. The animal who spoke up was right, the paint was so fresh, in fact, that it was still wet! This meant that his rump was now painted with a white ring from sitting on the wet toilet seat. He looked like he had a target on his rump! The moral of this story is that there are consequences to not being on time.

Another story I enjoy telling is about the Wildebeest. I rank Wildebeest as one of the least intelligent African animals. Migrating together in large numbers, one can hear them constantly making a grunting sound that sounds like they are repeatedly saying " no, no, no." In this story, the Wildebeest herd arrives at the edge of a river, and they restlessly line up in anticipation of making the crossing. The lead Wildebeest, who is very seasoned regarding migration, scouts the water and sees numerous Crocodiles waiting for the herd to start their river crossing. It is said that the lead animal sees the danger and shares warnings about Crocodiles with the rest of the herd. However, ignoring their leader, and thinking the Crocodiles are tree trunks or logs, the herd responds, "no, no, no" and starts jumping into the water. The outcome of the group is inevitable since only Crocodiles waited for them in the water. The moral of this story is to listen to the experienced leader.

The Wildebeest makes a second appearance in this next story. Most people are aware of Africa's Big Five, yet often are unaware that there is also an Ugly Five. This grouping includes the Hyena, Vulture, Warthog, Marabou Stork, and Wildebeest. Wildebeests are pretty strange in appearance. Legend shares that the Wildebeest was the last animal made by the creator. Exhausted and out of imaginative ideas, the creator decided to use all the leftover parts from the previously made animals. The leftover parts included the Buffalo's handlebar horns, the Grasshopper's long, flat head, the Cow's heavy body, the Lion's tufted tail, and the Goat's skinny legs. This explains it all!

The folklore story of the Tortoise and the Hare is one that is familiar to many people. But wait! There is another version that you may have yet to hear. One day, the Tortoise challenged the Hare to a race after growing tired of the Hare mocking him because he was so slow. The Hare knew how slow the Tortoise was, so he readily agreed. The Hare was so confident he would win the race that he began bragging to all that would listen. The Tortoise, acknowledging how slow he was, spoke to his family members about the race, and they devised a plan.

Their plan involved one Tortoise running the race while another went and hid close to the finishing line. The race started, and the Hare was quickly far ahead and out of sight of the Tortoise. With the final turn ahead, the Hare was sure that he would arrive at the finish line without any competition from the Tortoise. The Hare sauntered around the final turn but, to his dismay and confusion, saw the Tortoise crossing the finish line first. The Tortoise's plan had worked! To this day, the Hare remains baffled that he did not win and lost to one of the slowest creatures on the planet. The moral of this story is that with a bit of creative planning, anyone can achieve their goal.

I will leave you with one final story. When animals were created, several parts were made separately. The tail was one of these separate parts, and once created, they were left lying on the ground so the creator could quickly gather one when he wanted to add a tail to the creation. The day arrived for Humans and Monkeys to be created. The various types of Monkeys were built first before the creator moved on to con-

struct Humans. The plan was to create all the Humans and, once all were made, bring them over to the tail pile for their finishing touch. Each Human would be given the choice of a tail to add to themselves.

The Monkeys were curious about the pile of tails they found lying on the ground. Each Monkey decided to pick a tail that they felt suited themselves. Some picked short, stumpy ones, some picked tails that could grab onto branches and act like an extra hand or finger, and others chose long, flowing tails. All the Monkeys began to play with the tails when one suddenly stuck a tail on his behind. The other Monkeys thought this was a great idea, so they copied what that first Monkey did. The Monkeys played all day with their tails on their bottoms, only stopping when it was time for bed. Then, the Monkeys tried to remove the tails but found they could not! From that day forward, Monkeys have had tails.

Robala sentle—Sleep well.

9

LEOPARD ESCAPADES

One of NatHab's small, secluded camps is the Gomoti Camp, set in the 15,000-acre Santawani Private Concession. This concession is unique because it is owned by the local community, which ensures the local community benefits from the revenue generated by tourist activities. The camp is home to a waterhole directly in front of the main area and firepit. This waterhole attracts a steady stream of the wide variety of wildlife safari-goers crave, and this almost always guarantees the unexpected happening on those trips.

One morning, while on a game drive, the Gomoti Camp manager radioed me to share that a young female Leopard had just killed an Impala extremely close to guest tent number five. Of course, the guests wanted to turn around and return to the camp, hoping to spot the Leopard. When we arrived, we found the kill on the ground under an Acacia Tree, yet there was no sighting of the Leopard. After lingering a bit without a sighting, we proceeded with the day's activities.

Upon returning from our afternoon drive, we noticed the kill was still on the ground, and no Leopard was seen. An opportunistic predator will quickly take an abandoned kill. Certainly, I thought, the Hyenas would arrive to do so before we had to return to our tents for the night. Yet, when it was time for the guests to bed down for the night, the kill was still where it had been left this morning. No predator had come to claim it. We wondered what was happening; maybe the close proximity of Humans was the reason for this abnormality.

At midnight, after the camp was long asleep, the sound of a clan of Hyenas awakened me with their ruckus around my tent. I wondered if they had found the kill, but ultimately ignored them and went back to sleep. Walking to the main area in the morning, I saw drag marks and Hyena tracks littering the ground. Remembering my thoughts about the Hyenas and assuming they had come to collect the kill after we went to bed, I carried on with my typical morning routine without searching for the kill's new location. That day was the last day of the safari, and guests would fly home that evening. Once I dropped them off to catch their flights, I would have a few days to spend in my home city of Maun.

While in Maun, the Gomoti Camp manager called me for the second time in two days. He asked if I had noticed that the Impala carcass was gone. I told him I had but that I was unsure where it went. He shared that after a short search, he found it in a new location- the tree directly above my tent!

During the night, the Leopard finally returned to her kill, and, wanting to protect it from scavenging predators, she dragged it up the tree. This explained why the Hyenas sur-rounding my tent made such a commotion- they were trying to get to the kill. Then I realized I had walked out of my tent and broke a cardinal rule of safari guiding: always look side to side, forward and backward, and up before leaving your quar-ters. The Leopard could have been in the tree, and she could have viewed me as prey. I hate to think of what she could have done. While a scary thought, it reinforced for me a most mem-orable lesson: even though you cannot see an animal, they can see you.

This same female Leopard frequented the camp on other occasions as well. Early one morning before sunrise, I exited my tent and diligently scanned the still-dark surroundings with my flashlight while walking to the main area. I rounded a corner, and boom! There she was, reclined and completely relaxed on the side of the pathway. She was so close that I could have touched her if I wanted to. Instead, I froze in my steps. She, too, froze with her amber eyes locked on me. She showed no signs of aggression, only alertness. Moving to the opposite side of the walkway, I took a step forward to judge her reaction.

With each step, she continued to show no signs of aggres-sion. I kept walking and soon reached my destination with her amber eyes following me the entire way. As I reached the main area, she crossed over the pathway while moving closer to where I was going. Ignoring the Leopard, since she showed no signs of aggression leading me to feel safe, I went to the kitchen to get my morning tea. The female camp manager, Shadi, was already in the kitchen, so I told her to be alert as a Leopard was close to the main area. We walked together to see if she was still there, and I pointed out the young Leopard walking around.

By this time, I needed to leave to wake the guests. Upon my return, I found Shadi shining her flashlight around the area as she went about her work. As I watched, I noticed a prey-predator scenario unfolding. I watched Shadi move to a corner, and the very alert Leopard followed towards the same corner. When Shadi moved to another area, the Leopard did the same thing. Upon spotting me, the Leopard moved away. Shadi noticed me watching and asked me what I thought about what I had witnessed. Knowing I needed to be honest with her, I told her I felt the Leopard thought of her as prey, perhaps an Impala. It was Shadi's first face-to-face encounter with a Leopard, and she was so scared that she wanted to pack her bag and go home. Luckily for us, Shadi didn't!

Otsogile jang—How are you?

10

HUMAN ENCOUNTERS

The most common questions from guests are, "Aren't you tired of doing this repeatedly?" or "Do you ever get bored?" My answer is always a resounding NO! How could I? Every trip is different. You can see the same animal repeatedly; however, the situation or behavior won't be the same. This, combined with the opportunity to share my knowledge with new guests when they are experiencing things for the first time, is my passion. I take my responsibilities as an Expedition Guide very seriously, yet I typically feel no stress when out in the bush. Instead, stopping the vehicle, turning off the engine, and just sitting and watching wildlife is an instant stress reliever for me. Humans staring at wildlife. Wildlife staring at Humans. More often than not, wildlife goes about its activities and pays no attention to the big green animal (safari vehicle) with funny-looking moving "things" (People) inside it, pointing cameras and binoculars at them.

In addition to wildlife sightings, one of the most essential activities in the bush is creating time for yourself and the guests to fully absorb the surroundings. This means you can no longer look at your environment as one inclusive picture, but instead as a vast microcosm. Engaging as many senses as possible can enhance the experience. Look closely, and you can see the scars on the face of the majestic male Lion, the color variations of Giraffes, the spot pattern of a Leopard, the position of an Elephant's trunk, or even the play antiques of the Wild Dog puppies. Inhale deeply, and you could be engulfed in the smells of the wild. Listen intently to experience the sounds of a Fish Eagle calling, an Impala's alarm, an Elephant rum-

bling, a Lion's territorial call, or a Hippo's grunt. Let your skin feel the nature surrounding you through a soft breeze blowing, the rain falling from a sudden cloudburst, or the summer sun's heat.

Nature must be respected, meaning it needs to be treated like we borrowed it from someone. Many of my first-time safari guests have a limited understanding of nature and the African bush. Probably the most essential part of my job is to share my knowledge, teach guests, and create 'wow' moments while they open themselves to experiences they never even thought about. However, sharing my knowledge and experiences goes further than sharing wildlife information. Helping guests understand the impact of their actions while out on a drive is equally important. Most guests get excited when we come upon an exciting sighting. With this excitement often comes the 'oohs and aahs' spoken in raised voices or the desire to stand up in the vehicle to get a better look. Once I explain the reason for speaking softly and remaining seated at all times, most guests understand, respect, and listen to my instructions.

Now and then, there will be a difficult guest. Perhaps they do not want to rotate vehicle seats to ensure all guests get various views. Maybe it is the refusal to adhere to the safety regulations for remaining seated, potentially jeopardizing all guests' safety. I am responsible for addressing these personalities and safety issues quickly and efficiently.

While leading an expedition, my hands are full, and I carry the responsibility for the well-being and safety of the guests on my shoulders. Should any harm come to a guest, the first person with a finger pointed at them will be me. It is crucial as a guide to establish a relationship of trust and respect with my guests and for guests to remember it is a two-way street. Their life could depend upon this.

I do not have many requirements for my guests. However, I do insist upon respect for each other, respect for safari and camp staff, and respect for nature. What this means is that rudeness is left back home. My mantra is to leave rudeness back home and to bring respect with you. If you do this, I will salute you. If you bring rudeness, I will keep you at a distance. If the rudeness is extreme or escalates, I will give the individual only one warning to cease and desist.

Fortunately, I have not had many experiences with disrespectful guests, but unfortunately, it has happened before. I remember one guest on a safari who was so rude to me and the other guests that it became a serious problem. I warned him that I would remove him from the safari if he continued with this behavior. At this, he challenged me. With a demeaning stare, he said, "That won't happen. Do you know how much I paid for this trip?" I told him I didn't know or care, as accepting rude behavior is not part of my job and was unfair to the other guests. He did not respond to my comment. We went our separate ways and went to our tents for the night. I hoped he would sleep on it and join the group the next day with a better attitude.

Boy, was I wrong! The next day, his behavior worsened, which I did not even think was possible. The guests were noticeably uncomfortable; some were even distressed by his behavior. Knowing he was now disrupting the safari for the rest of the guests, I had to take additional action. I called the tour company's office, knowing they had a zero-tolerance policy for disruptive guests. The office immediately decided to terminate the remainder of the individual's trip, and arrangements were made to fly him out the same day. Angered, the guest approached me and said he would not leave a tip for me or any other camp staff. I replied that it was fine since we always appreciated tips, but neither the team nor I relied on tips. He gathered his belongings, climbed into the vehicle, and I drove him to the airstrip. It was a long, silent trip, as we had no conversation during the ride. He exited the vehicle and entered the plane without a goodbye.

Arriving back at camp, I was greeted warmly by the remaining guests. They said what I did showed them I could remain calm under pressure and that I clearly had the best interest of the entire group in hand. They all shared that they were glad to see him leave and would back my actions when it came time to complete their trip evaluation. After every trip, I received a report of the guests' feedback. I expected to receive a very negative report from the dismissed guest, but it never came! I like to think he thought about the series of events and realized that his behavior caused his trip to be cut short. Somehow, I doubt this, though.

Although more common, it is not only guests that can cause challenges during a trip. I worked with different agents worldwide, which allowed me to experience all the camps throughout Botswana. Unknown to many, I am the only Botswana native Expedition Leader who speaks fluent German and works under the Wilderness umbrella. Because of this, I am frequently asked to lead German and Swiss safaris through Zambia and Botswana. On one of my Swiss departures, we stayed in a camp in the Okavango Delta. Upon camp arrival, we were greeted by an English-speaking South African couple who managed the camp. In addition to the couple, there was a local manager who was responsible for the primary interactions with the guests. Since my guests did not speak English, I needed to translate and ensure my guests were comfortable. This included requesting private seating for meals so that the guests would feel comfortable speaking German throughout their meals. The South African couple did not like my request. However, the local manager understood the reason and honored it anyway.

After the trip ended, I was called into the local office, where the operations manager handed me an email from the English-speaking camp managers. The email contained the complaint that I only spoke German to communicate with guests, which they found very rude. I let out a full belly laugh, looked at the operations manager, and asked him what was next. He, too, laughed, knowing the whole story, and sent me on my way to enjoy my days off before my next trip.

The next trip was also with German-speaking guests, and our last camp during this trip happened to be the same one that the English-speaking couple ran. I was prepared to hear what they would say to me when we arrived, expecting complaints similar to those in their emails after the last trip. Yet, the couple said nothing. Instead, they watched my every move.

One day, as I do for every evening game drive, I packed my cooler box for the sundown drinks (amarula, gin & tonic, beers, wine, and soft drinks) that the guests would enjoy. When we returned to camp, I brought the cooler box to the bar, as I always do, to be unpacked, and I left to walk the guests to their rooms. Later, the barman shared that when I left, the couple rushed to the bar and asked him to be sure all the drinks were accounted for. When questioned why, they told him they needed to be sure I was not taking alcoholic drinks back to my tent. Knowing this was a strange request, the barman asked why they thought I would take alcoholic beverages to my tent. They told him they did not trust me because I spoke German to the guests, and they were left out of the conversations. The barman had my back and promptly shared that he knew me very well and had never seen me have any alcohol. He spoke the absolute truth- I never partake in anything that could alter my alertness or perception when I am guiding. I take the responsibility for the safety of my guests as one of my primary jobs.

From that day forward, the couple made it a point to avoid all interactions with me. To this day, they even go as far as swapping their camp assignment with other camp managers when they know I will be arriving. I'm still following my life's chosen path, and my patience has brought me where I am now. Without it, I would not have endured the tough times with guests, camp managers and staff, and agents who have crossed my path as a professional Expedition Leader.

Goroga sentle—Arrive Safely

11

HEART RACING

As I shared in an earlier chapter, exploring and interacting with nature is my favorite thing to do. Yet, during bush encounters, there have been times when I wondered if I should continue doing what I'm doing or change my career for something a bit tamer. However, my Brother, Dad, and Uncle taught and showed me that if you had a job or career you enjoy or, better yet, are passionate about, you should continue in that work. They did this until they passed away, their lives not taken by their work industries, but by their maker. Watching my own children develop their love of wildlife, I know I have set the same good example for them that my family did for me. Should they choose to follow a similar career path to me, I would readily support them. For these reasons I think it is important that I continue on my career journey no matter the encounter or experience.

Thinking that wildlife encounters only happen while you are on a game drive is foolish. They happen in towns, in camps, and even on airstrips. The concessions, private preserves, and camps we travel through do not have fences. This gives the wildlife freedom to move about during the day and night. Knowing this, we must never forget that we, the humans, are intruders. The wildlife was in the area long before the safari trips began.

Whenever you are out in nature, the keyword to remember is always respect. The more we respect nature and all it brings, the more it will respect us. Occasionally, regardless of how respectful of nature one is, encounters with dangerous animals do occur. This does not necessarily mean you did something irresponsible or reckless. Sometimes, these encounters are purely by chance and without your prior awareness or knowledge.

For example, one night, I walked from the camp's main area to my tent after dropping guests at their tents to settle for the evening. As I walked the path to my tent, I noticed a shadow moving towards me from the opposite direction. While I noticed the shadow's movement, the shadow did not appear to notice mine. Not concerned, I continued down the path and rounded a sharp corner. Boom! There, directly in front of me, staring eye-to-eye, was a large male Lion. I stopped abruptly, my flashlight beam shining straight into his massive face. Unblinking amber eyes stared back. A rush of warmth passed through my body, and my heart beat so fast and loudly that I was sure the Lion could hear it. Remembering the rule of the bush, "whatever you do, don't run," I began thinking, how do I get out of this situation? What are my options?

I thought about shouting but was concerned this might startle the Lion and make him aggressive. I considered, then reconsidered, throwing my flashlight at him, since doing so would leave me in the darkness. I decided that my best option was to back away slowly. I took a step backward while keeping my eyes on the Lion. There was no movement from the Lion. Another step. Still no movement, just a continuous stare from the Lion. Slowly, I backed around the corner, and with one last glance, I turned and bolted, full speed, back to the main area. Searching for cover, I jumped in the LandRover safari vehicle, where I was determined to stay until I saw the Lion pass by. I was even prepared to spend the night there if I never saw him walk past. Luckily, after a few minutes, I saw him saunter by, scanning from side to side as he walked—I wondered if he was looking for me. Realizing my heart was still pumping fast, I took a deep breath to help calm myself down, and once calm, I thanked God for protecting me in that scary situation.

Another heart racing example came from a journey to Semetse Camp, situated along the Boro River that demarcates Chief's Island and Ntswi Village in the Okavango Delta. Chief's Island, the largest of the islands in the Okavango Delta, was once the private hunting preserve of the local chief. Our camp was situated under beautiful trees that provided much-needed cooling shade. The trees were also fruit-bearing, and the fruit was among the favorites of Elephants. One afternoon, having some spare time, I decided to nap in my dome tent. I was tired enough, so I crawled in and promptly fell asleep. After an hour or so, the sound of something breaking branches and tearing foliage from the trees outside my tent awakened me.

It was so hot that day that I had left the entrance to the tent open to allow a breeze to flow through. Looking out the opening, I saw a massive Elephant walking quite close to the tent and towards the looming shading trees. As the Elephant slowly moved, it shook a tree, and falling fruit bombarded my tent. It was then that I noticed the tent, being so small, was almost entirely under the Elephant's front quarters. I knew that with any given step, the Elephant could crush my tent and me with it. The Elephant could also lift and toss my tent aside if they decided it was in their way. With these realizations, fear began to set in.

I knew I needed to get as far away from the Elephant and my tent as quickly as possible. Gathering my courage, I swiftly

crawled out of the tent's opening, darted through the Elephant's legs, and disappeared into the closest bush. Luckily, the Elephant was so busy enjoying the fruits that my escape went unnoticed. I didn't even tell my guests that afternoon what had happened. No safari-goer wants to hear that their Expedition Leader was scared, or in danger!

I will leave you with one more heart racing story, although there are plenty more I could mention. In each camp, the Expedition Leader is responsible for walking from tent-to-tent in pitch darkness to wake the guests up every morning.

The African night is starry yet very dark. Unlike at my guests' home, there is no ambient light like that found from street lamps or business signs, and having a moonless night makes it even darker. Therefore, early morning wake-up calls, when the sun has not yet risen, can be scary despite carrying a powerful flashlight. In one of our camps, these wake-up calls involved making my way along the boardwalk that ran from my tent to the guests' tents. Along the way, I would pass sizable Leadwood Trees with beautiful branches that created a canopy over the boardwalk. I always enjoyed walking under the Leadwood Tree canopy; it often felt like nature was enveloping me with its strong arms.

One particular morning, after waking the guests, I returned to my tent to collect my gear for the morning drive and then headed back along the boardwalk to place my gear in the vehicle. As I approached the first of the Leadwood Trees, I saw something strange that I had not noticed when I had previously walked to wake the guests. Moving closer and aiming my flashlight to inspect the area, I immediately identified a blood stain, a fresh blood stain! I spun around quickly, shining my flashlight and checking the surrounding area for whatever animal had left it. Finding nothing on the ground, I swung the light beam into the canopy branch directly above me. There, not more than twenty feet above, was a female Leopard lying on the canopy branch with a fresh Impala kill. She paused, meeting my gaze, and then returned to enjoying her early morning feast. It is not every day that a person comes in such close contact with a Leopard eating her fresh kill. Initially startled from this encounter, my heart rate slowly returned to normal after noticing she was not viewing me as a threat.

Once she had her fill and the sun had come up, she climbed down from the tree and wandered off into the bush, leaving the remains of the Impala securely lodged in the tree, surely with plans to return to her feast again when she was hungry. It was obvious that she had already been there when I passed by to wake the guests and I had missed her. Over breakfast, my guests shared their shock as I recounted my early morning adventure. They could not understand how I could walk under the canopy without realizing a Leopard was enjoying her breakfast just above! The important lesson here? While we do not always see the animals, they always see us!

Goithokomela—Take care

12

THE BUSH IS CALLING

Nature is incredible in such a variety of ways that one cannot understand it completely. When you combine the wide variety of animals, flora, fauna, environments, people, etc, that nature is composed of, one can not help but wonder how this has been made possible. When I ask the people in my groups why they have chosen to travel such long distances to Botswana, I inadvertently always hear, "Why to see the "Big 5" of course!" By this, they mean that they want to see Lions, Leopards, Rhinoceroses, Elephants, and African Buffalo. The Big 5 are identified not for their size, but for their perceived danger and coveted worth among game hunters. However, let me be very clear, I do not condone ANY type of game hunting for sport.

While I understand the desire to see the Big 5, there is so much more to Botswana besides these animals. As the Expedition Leader, I am responsible for educating and broadening guest knowledge. For example, many are unfamiliar with the

"Little 5" and the "Ugly 5." The Little 5 is the phrase coined for the group of small mammals and insects whose names contain the names of the Big 5. The phrase came about after the successful marketing of the Big 5 phrase to safari-goers. The Little 5 are the Elephant Shrew, Ant Lion, Rhinoceros Beetle, Buffalo Weaver, and the Leopard Tortoise. Also not to be overlooked, the Ugly 5, aptly named for their appearance, are the Hyena, Marabou Stork, Vulture, Warthog, and Wildebeest.

Even beyond animals, there is so much more that makes a trip to Botswana unforgettable. Identifying the multitude of animal tracks, the sounds of animal calls at night and during the day, birds and their melodious calls, varying insects, reptiles, and the wide variety of dung and scat scattered everywhere.

While on the subject, a word about dung and scat. While many use the two words interchangeably, they are not the same. Dung is from animals that graze on grasses and foliage, whereas scat is from those that feed on meat. For example, Elephants produce dung- and lots of it! Where Lions and Leopards produce scat.

As you may be able to tell, I get excited when I have guests interested in things beyond the Big 5. I call them "my safari people". There is nothing that can beat the bush while sitting around the bush TV with my safari people, enjoying a glass of GNT (Gin & Tonic), and listening to the sounds of nature; a Lion's roar, the Hyenas' laughing, a Leopard's deep, guttural rasping call, Hippos' grunting, and Elephants trumpeting, all traveling miles through the night. Looking up, one also sees the African night sky blanketed with millions of stars unseen in the cities and towns that my guests come from. Combining all of this can change a trip from a so-so trip to a great one, which I translate into an unforgettable safari experience.

Moso o montle—Lovely morning

13

HIPPO LEGEND AND HAPPENSTANCE

According to the legend of the Hippo, all living creatures were created to live on land. Struggling with this, Hippos went to the Creator to share their concerns. They said, "Creator, with all due respect, we can't live on land because we have very sensitive skin, and the sun burns us badly when we are on land." The Creator shared their own concerns and responded, "You are so big. If you live in the water, you will surely eat up all the other organisms living there!" The Hippos tried to compromise and said, "If you allow us to spend our time in the water, we will not eat while in there." Not convinced, the Creator asked, "How can I be sure you are not feeding on any living creature in water?" The Hippos asked to be given two weeks to prove themselves. "We promise to open our mouths wide in an enormous yawn often so you can check to see if any fishtails are stuck in there. We also promise to expose our hindquarters

and spread our dung so that you can search for any bones."

As the weeks passed by, the Creator continued checking the Hippo's mouths and dung. Finally, finding nothing amiss, the Creator permanently allowed the Hippos to live in the water during the day and return to land in the evening to feed while the sun was down.

Hippos, known as one of the largest animals, are also among the most dangerous. They kill more Humans than any other African animal. What many do not know is that Hippos do not swim when in the water. Instead, they walk along the river's bottom bed. Despite their size and dangerous reputation, Hippos are strict vegetarians.

On one occasion, I was doing a Mokoro activity at Semetsi Camp, located along the Boro River, one of the boundaries of Chiefs Island. Chief's Island, the largest Okavango Delta island, is set in the center of the Delta. It got its name as it was the private hunting reserve of Chief Moremi of the local Batawana tribe. This is the same camp where I previously shared that my afternoon nap was disturbed by a foraging Elephant.

I set off early in the morning, sharing the Mokoro with one guest and one poler, as I was not yet fully competent being the only poler. From a young age, elders teach polers to stay close to the water banks, as that is the safest area from which they can see animals in the water and create an easy escape to dryland or shallow water if needed.

Less than one-half a mile from camp that morning, we had to cross the deep main channel to get to a smaller channel on the other side. As the poler reached the middle of the main channel, a large Hippo popped up from under the water, not more than a few feet, to the side of our Mokoro. I turned and looked at the poler, clearly seeing his legs shaking and a worried look on his face. This exact situation was why polers avoided the middle deep channels.

To further add to our precarious situation, a strong channel current was drifting us closer to the Hippo. The seriousness of the situation spread to the guests, who remained silent. Spotting us, the Hippo quickly submerged back into the deep water. The water, being so clear, enabled us to see that the Hippo was coming towards us. We watched the Hippo disappear under the Mokoro and held our breath, wondering if he would emerge while flipping us into the air. Looking around, I pondered where we might land if this happened.

Luckily, the Hippo must not have perceived us as a threat and had no intention of hitting our Mokoro. Silently, he passed underneath, popped up on the other side, and, without looking back, continued to move away from us. Loud sighs of relief were heard across our Mokoro since we all knew how dangerous Hippos can be. They have been known to chase boats or Mokoro if they feel threatened. We were so scared, and it was truly a close encounter.

Hippos—Kubu

14

BUSH DISORIENTATION

I have experienced a lot during my journeys in the bush, with both the wildlife and the guests. Every guest is different, so I have traveled with many types of guests. Some guests are mammal lovers, some are bird lovers, some enjoy flora and fauna, and some are intimidated by the animals altogether. Some guests have decreased hearing or mobility, some are happy regardless of what they are doing, and some have a personality only a mother could love. Irrespective of their likes, I enjoy the presence of each of my guests and what they bring to an expedition.

I am confident in my skills and rarely become frightened during my journeys. Yet occasionally, a situation arises that causes my heart rate to speed up- like some of the stories we covered earlier. However, sometimes these heart racing moments have more to do with my guests than anything else. I remember one time in particular when I was truly alarmed regarding a guest. On every morning game drive, we take a break to stretch our legs and enjoy a tea or coffee break. This tea break is often along the Linyanti River. The river, a permanent water source that forms the border between Botswana and Namibia, is a pristine area with Hippos scattered throughout the water, Crocodiles basking in the sun on the river's edge, and a wide variety of other animals frequently visiting to drink.

These tea breaks are often the time for guests to "check the tires," which, on my safaris, is a code term for using the bush bathroom or loo. During one of the tea breaks that morning, a guest informed me she would like to "check the tires," so I found her a safe area, with a big Leadwood Tree for privacy, about fifteen yards away from the vehicle. Off she went. I made myself busy making tea and coffee for the other guests while they enjoyed watching the Hippos and Crocodiles scattered about the river. Five minutes passed when I noticed the bush loo guest had not yet returned. Another minute passed, and there was still no sign of her. I asked another female guest if she would check on the missing woman. She agreed and began calling the missing loo guest by her name, but, unfortunately, she did not get a response. She walked around the Leadwood Tree, which was meant to offer privacy to the woman, only to find no sign of the bush loo guest. Hurrying back to the group, she told me what had happened. The bush loo guest had vanished!

Unsure what was going on, I asked all the guests to return to the safety of our vehicle while I went to look for our missing companion. I rushed to the Leadwood Tree and began looking for her footprint tracks.

Tracking, an invaluable skill for anyone out in the bush, was taught to me by my Grandfather when I was a herd boy looking after his livestock. When a Cow went missing, he would show me how to track it, how to tell what direction it went in, whether it was walking or running, and whether the tracks were new or old. Along the way, he also pointed out the other animal tracks of those living in his fields such as Hare, Aardvark, and Porcupines. My tracking skills were fine-tuned during my Expedition Leader course because of this.

My guest's tracks, which were easy to find, indicated she headed off in the direction opposite the vehicle. Calling her name, I got no response. As I said, I am confident in my ability to keep my guests safe, and I rarely become frightened. Yet I admit, my heart rate sped up a bit that morning as the guest remained missing.

As mentioned earlier, there is a rule in the bush that says, "Whatever you do in the bush, do not run." But, that morning, I found myself running after our lost guest's tracks. I was worried because I knew the preserve area attracted large herds of Elephants, often coming to the river to drink. While Elephants appear relaxed and gentle, mothers, and maternal herds in general, are very protective of their young and will not hesitate to defend against anything that they perceive to be a threat to them. A bull (male) Elephant in musth, a periodic time of high male hormone testosterone levels, is often unpredictable and can be very aggressive. I hoped my guest did not encounter either of these scenarios.

After searching for more than five minutes, I saw a movement out of the corner of my eye. Running towards the termite mound where I saw the movement, I finally spotted my guest. I asked her, "Where are you going?" Startled at seeing me, she explained frantically that she was looking for her group and the vehicle she had been riding in. She was so frightened that she did not even recognize me. We walked back to the vehicle together. As soon as we arrived, I noticed tears of relief running down her face.

I shared with the group what I will share with you all now. This was not the first time a guest became disoriented during a journey. That day, we spoke about some ways they could potentially decrease that happening in the future. Look around at your surroundings; look for landmarks such as the river, trees, and bushes, and take note of them. We discussed how, if the river is on your right going to the bush loo, it will be on your left returning to the group. I often wondered about that incident and how many of those guests decided they would not have to use the bush loo again after it happened.

Gotimela—Getting lost

15

EARTH RUMBLES

The Cape to Cairo route is the longest route on one of my itineraries. This route runs from the western corner of Silinda Spillway to the Savuti Marsh. The Spillway, called Magwegquana in the local language, is located in Botswana's remote western region, an often dry channel that connects Linyanti Swamps and the Okavango Delta. The Savuti Marsh, located in Chobe National Park, consists of over 4,000 square miles of grassland teeming with wildlife.

I always warn my guests that travel between the two areas will be a long, arduous, full day of driving over often bumpy and rutted dirt roads. I also ensure I inform the guests that we would be leaving our camp at 6 a.m., and they should mentally plan on arriving at our next camp eleven to twelve hours later. I then ensure to add that the drive would provide an incredible wildlife viewing opportunity, so we would take our time and stop should the viewing warrant it.

In general, guests could expect to see large concentrations of Elephants gathering at the waterholes wallowing in mud, enjoying a relaxing "swim," or satisfying their thirst. The younger Elephants may be practicing their "charges" and how to use their trunks. Perhaps the guests would see a pride of Lions spending their time ambushing baby Elephants that wandered away or those left behind by the herd. They may see the protective corralling of the young by a herd of Elephants when a baby is threatened. However, although exciting, Elephants and Lions were not the only wildlife they could expect to see.

For example, we came across a stunning young female Leopard on an afternoon of a Cape to Cairo drive. We spent the remainder of the afternoon with her, and it was after sunset when we arrived at our campsite, and the guests dispersed to their small tents to freshen up. Remember, this was an adventure camp safari, so freshening up is a relative term, and my guests accomplished it by using a small water basin in front of their tents.

I took this time to check in with the kitchen crew to discuss the time for dinner. As I talked to the crew, we heard a loud rumble of thunder that traveled through the ground, shaking our feet. Looking toward the sky, the chef shared his confusion, "Why is there thunder, yet the sky is blue, and no clouds can be seen?" I, on the other hand, knew immediately what this was. I replied that it was an earthquake. I turned around and saw my guests freeze as they, too, did not know what was happening. Unknown to the guests, Botswana has its share of earthquakes, yet they are rarely felt because of the depth of sand in the region. I shared the information with the guests, and armed with this knowledge, we all continued our activities.

About fifteen minutes later, a guest spotted an animal in our camp and was unsure what it was since he couldn't see it clearly. He wondered if it could be a Hyena. Looking in the direction he was pointing, I quickly identified that it was not a Hyena but the young female Leopard we had seen on our afternoon drive. Of course, that raised the question, "How can you be so sure it is the same Leopard?" Taking this as an opportunity to educate, I shared that Leopards can be identified by the spot patterns found above their top whiskers. This spot pattern remains consistent throughout a Leopard's lifetime and can vary from one spot to more above the whiskers and from side-to-side. Some will have a pattern referred to as 3:3, meaning three spots on both sides of their face, or perhaps 3:1, three spots on one side and one spot on the other.

I encouraged the guests to speak softly and quietly so she would stick around and not run away. Soon, as she continued to linger cautiously, it became clear to us that the Leopard was scared. Most likely, she had never experienced an earthquake during her young life. Restlessly, our Leopard companion paced between the tents before eventually settling down near the kitchen tent only a few yards away from us. She remained there, seated with us while we enjoyed our dinner. We all assumed she would move on after dinner and settle elsewhere for the night. However, our young Leopard friend had other plans, as she ended up spending the entire night at our campsite.

Feeling braver during the night, she seemed to have seized the opportunities presented to her. In the morning, guests

reported hearing our Leopardess hunting the small creatures, most likely mice, that scurried between their tents. Our Leopard moved on from the camp sometime in the early hours, and we never spotted her again.

Bontle tota—Amazing

16

THUNDER SEASON

During the Botswana rainy season, which stretches from November through March, thunderstorms occur late in the afternoons, evenings, and even into early nighttime, sometimes challenging sleep. One day, I was in the Kalahari Game Reserve leading a group of seven guests on a mobile safari. Late one afternoon, while on a game drive, large, towering, and menacing-looking thunderhead clouds started to build up in the east. We all decided we needed to head back to the campsite before we got caught by the impending storm. As soon as we arrived back at our site, it started to rain softly, accompanied by bright flashes of lightning, and followed by loud crashing booms of thunder. The guests and I were relaxing in the central gathering area tent, enjoying the light and sound show that Mother Nature was putting on for us.

After watching for about thirty minutes, there was a notable change in the air. The rain changed from gentle to wind-driven. The wind's strength continued to pick up to where the poles holding the dinner tent began to topple. We quickly rushed to the toppled poles, trying (in vain) to hold the tent corners up in support. It was a heroic effort, but we could not win against the wind. Soon, the entire dinner tent blew away! We were all soaked. We turned to see where the dome tents were set up. Some stood firm, but the majority had toppled and some even blew away. A storm this strong was not something we had planned for. Luckily, during the rainy season, we always had the top on the safari vehicle, so we all ran to take cover there until the storm passed much later that evening.

While hunkered down in the vehicle, reality sunk in. We abandoned everything when we took cover, and everyone got wet running to the vehicle. We had yet to prepare dinner. I worried about where the guests would sleep because all of the tent bedding was soaked, if there was even a tent there at all. Since this was a mobile safari, there was no extra supply of bedding or dome tents. My 'Expedition Leader's problem-solving mind' clicked into overdrive. For dinner, we feasted on fruits, cereal, and beverages that were still in the vehicle from our game drive. I brought out the fleece-lined ponchos we carry in the vehicle for the guests to use as bedding. Those whose tents remained intact shared what they could with the less fortunate guests. The tents that had blown down but were still around were gathered and quickly put back up.

Even with these quick solutions, I am sure it was a long night for the guests as several spent the night on the ground with only the borrowed ponchos. Yet, despite all this, they did not complain. They understood that flexibility and compromise were necessary out in the bush and could limit how difficult things could become.

I always think it is important to note that thunderstorms can highlight a variety of emotions for many. Some guests love a "good storm" and want to capture pictures of the lightning electrifying the sky. The sound of thunder scares others, and they jump every time. Others come with family beliefs and rituals surrounding thunderstorms.

One guest shared that as a child, she watched her mother take holy water and sprinkle some in each room of the house. This ritual was meant to bless the house and keep it safe from being struck by lightning.

As a child, I remember our house being struck by lightning. My Mum told me this happened because my Dad was sound asleep on his back. This was just one of many beliefs that she had. My Mum also performed rituals when a storm was brewing, including going around our home and covering all the mirrors. She covered the mirrors because some believe that mirrors could trap evil spirits during a storm.

As an adult, I never sit and watch lightning, since I had the traumatic experience of witnessing someone get struck by lightning only a few yards away from me. This happened when

I was twenty- six and working at Semetsi Camp in the Okavango Delta. While there are small grocery stands in each
village, the villagers often have to travel to Maun to obtain
additional supplies. To do so, they must cross the Boro River
via Mokoro to get to the vehicle that will bring them into
Maun, and do the reverse with their supplies on the return.

My guests and I were enjoying our afternoon tea along-
side the Boro River before departing on a planned boat cruise
one day. We relaxed while watching the villagers return from
their supply trip. Storm clouds were beginning to form, so the
villagers placed their goods underneath a large tree nearby to
prevent them from getting wet if it started raining. We have all
been taught not to stand near trees when there is lightning, yet
none had been seen. Suddenly, a lightning bolt flashed down
from the clouds and struck a village lady close to the tree. It
happened so quickly that what had been a relaxing afternoon tea time for my guests and me, quickly turned into a
nightmare.

Setsuwetsuwe—Thunderstorm

17

LIFE & DEATH IN NATURE

Being in nature often gives you some incredible and memorable experiences that are forever etched in my heart. Throughout my 18 years of guiding, I have seen so much happen in the bush. One of the most unbelievable experiences I had was on a mobile camping trip in the Kalahari. I had six guests on my trip, and we stayed three nights at a HATAB site. A HATAB site is a camp that is a member of the Hospitality and Tourism Association of Botswana and, as such, is certified to meet the high industry standards.

Our activities on this trip included the typical morning-afternoon game drives. On the second morning drive, as we headed in the open plains of Deception Valley, we saw Springboks and Oryx, also known as Gemsboks, bunched together and facing in one direction. We heard several Springboks emitting noises that sounded like a combination of a bark and grunt. I explained to the group that this was the Springbok's warning call which they emit to warn the rest of the group when danger is sensed or identified in the area. This told me there must be a predator nearby, or at least somewhere along the ridge. I told my guests to be patient and wait to see if they could spot the predator in the surroundings. After almost ten minutes, the Springboks and Oryx started moving toward our vehicle while still concentrating on something in the distance.

I pulled out my binoculars to scan the area and soon spotted two male Cheetahs approaching the Antelopes from about thirty yards away. Within the next minute, the chase was on! Antelopes scattered in every direction, with some running towards our vehicle. The Cheetahs happened to turn their focus to those now running towards us.

As the panicked Antelopes reached the front of our vehicle, one decided to turn sharply to the right. Unfortunately, that would prove to be a fatal mistake. He had turned right into the Cheetah, who was attempting to cut its prey off from the rest of the herd. I called that scene a collision, not a kill. This is because the Cheetahs and Antelope collided in such a way that we couldn't see what was happening. A large dust cloud arose from the area. The guests began to clammer behind me, "Oh my goodness, God…, oh my God, Richard, what happened? We can't see anything!" My response was to wait for the dust cloud to clear. As the dust slowly dissipated, we saw the two Cheetahs with their front paws on top of the Springbok. My guests quickly realized that the Springbok was no longer alive.

Turning to my guests, I asked what they thought of what they had just witnessed? Many were amazed. However, I noticed one of my guests had thrown his poncho over his head. I approached the guest and asked him what was wrong. He shared that we just saw the one thing he had hoped he would never see! While he did not mind seeing animals eating their kills, he did not want to see one animal being killed by another. Later that day, he said he would not join the group on our afternoon game drive. He disclosed that he was concerned we might encounter another scene resulting in death. He did not want to witness the reality that animals need to eat, and predators need to kill to survive.

Botshelo bo a dikologa—Circle of Life

18

COLLECTIVE NAMES FOR GROUPS OF ANIMALS

We are all familiar with terms such as a pride of Lions or a herd of Elephants. Did you know there are some unique names given to groups of African animals. How many of these are you familiar with?

Antelope: a herd

Ants: a colony or an army

Apes: a shrewdness

Baboons: a troop or congress

Badgers: a cete

Bats: a colony, cloud or cauldron

Bees: a swarm

Buffalo: a gang or obstinacy

Cats: a clowder, glaring, pounce, nuisance or clutter; Wild cats: a destruction

Cheetahs: a coalition

Cranes: a sedge

Crocodiles: a float or bask

Dogs: a pack or cowardice; Puppies: a litter

Eagles: a convocation

Elephants: a herd, parade or memory

Flamingos: a stand or flamboyance

Foxes: a skulk

Frogs: an army or a colony

Hares: a down or husk

Hawks: a cast or kettle

Hippopotami: a bloat, bloat, or thunder

Hounds: a pack, mute or cry

Hyenas: a cackle or clan

Leopards: a leap

Lions: a pride

Monkeys: a barrel, cartload, or troop

Mongoose: a band

Otters: a family, romp or raft

Owls: a parliament

Porcupines: a prickle

Rabbits: a colony or warren

Rhinoceroses: a crash

COLLECTIVE NAMES FOR GROUPS OF ANIMALS

Snakes: a nest or knot

Squirrels: a dray or scurry

Storks: a mustering

Turtles: a bale or nest

Vultures: a venue or committee

Warthogs: a sounder

Wasps: a pledge

Wildebeest: a confusion or implausibility

Zebras: a zeal or dazzle

19

TEST YOUR KNOWLEDGE

QUESTIONS

Answers found on pages 104–109.

QUESTION	TRUE OR FALSE
1. Animals communicate in multiple ways.	
2. Lions hunt more during the day than at night.	
3. The Hippopotamus is one of the Big Five.	
4. Lion vocalization is exclusive to roaring.	

Question	True or False
5. The knobs on the top of Giraffes' heads are called spikes.	
6. Ostriches can run up to 45 mph.	
7. Hippos spray or fan their poop.	
8. Leopards pair for life.	
9. The Lion's whiskers are longer and more numerous than all the African Cats.	
10. Impala poop is called dung.	
11. Baby Meerkats are called pups.	
12. Only male Lions roar.	
13. Elephants have 4,000 muscles in their trunk.	
14. A Giraffe's tongue is dark blue/purple.	
15. Adult Lions typically feed every 2-4 days.	
16. Elephant sweat glands are located under their ears.	

Question	True or False
17. Impala are called the Bush MacDonalds because of their impressive high numbers	
18. The Baobab Tree is also known as the Tree of Life.	
19. The Bush people of the Kalahari Desert are called the Maasai.	
20. Bushbucks are among the smallest Antelopes found throughout Africa.	
21. The Marabou Stork is the only bird to have two toes.	
22. A Leopard's spots are called rosettes.	
23. A Cheetah's toe claws are not retractable.	
24. A Hyena's "laugh" travels further than a Lion's roar.	
25. On average, a male Lion hunts for 7-9 hours per day.	

Compare your answers to those on the following pages.

Answers:

1.	Animals communicate in multiple ways.	**True** Communication also occurs through body structures, posture, scent, facial expressions, and other body language, to name a few.
		Body structures: male Lions with darker manes have higher testosterone levels, which supports increased strength; their overall body size and size of the horns can identify the most dominant Kudu.
		Posture: can tell us if an animal is relaxed, frightened, dominant, submissive, agitated, or aggressive.
		Body language: bared teeth, pinned-back ears, raised tail, head down, and a low crouch often signal aggression or impending attack. A relaxed, open-mouthed expression with forward-facing ears shows contentment or curiosity.
		Facial expressions: can signal relaxation, fear, alertness, curiosity, or impending aggression.
		Scent: scents and scent marking can communicate territory, fear, defense, or readiness to mate.
2.	Lions hunt more during the day than at night.	**True** Lions are diurnal, however, they will adapt to nocturnal and twilight hunting if needed for survival.

3.	The Hippopotamus is one of the Big Five.	**False** The Big Five, named not for their size but for game hunting difficulty and desirability, are Lion, Rhinoceros, Elephant, Leopard, and Buffalo. (NOTE: I do not condone or support game hunting.)
4.	Lion vocalization is exclusive to roaring.	**False** Lions have a wide variety of vocalizations, including: *Roars:* multifunction vocalization primarily used to declare territory or to locate pride members over long distances (contact calling). *Grunts:* used for close-range communication; heard during social interactions within the pride. *Growls:* often signifies a more aggressive stance; typically used when a Lion feels threatened or during confrontations over food or territory. *Purrs and Meows:* used by mothers to communicate with their cubs; less intense sounds that are crucial in bonding and soothing the young ones.

5.	The knobs on the top of Giraffes' heads are called spikes.	**False** The knobs are called ossicones and are covered with skin and fur. They are used to differentiate between the sexes. Males: larger, thicker, smooth topped. Females: thinner with a tuft of hair on the top.
6.	Ostriches can run up to 45 mph.	**True** Ostriches hold the record for being the fastest on land, the largest, and the heaviest bird.
7.	Hippos spray or fan their poop.	**True** Hippos scatter their poop by fanning their tails to mark their territory.
8.	Leopards pair for life.	**False** Leopards are solitary cats that only come together to mate.
9.	The Lion's whiskers are longer and more numerous than all the African cats.	**False** The Leopard's whiskers are as wide as its body and are a constant supply of information that helps with navigating their environment.
10.	Impala poop is called dung.	**True** Impalas are herbivores; therefore, they produce dung. Scat is produced by carnivores.
11.	Baby Meerkats are called pups.	**True** Born in litters of 1-8, they are blind, deaf, nearly hairless, and weigh less than 2 ounces.

12.	Only male Lions roar.	**False** While more common in males, females use it when communicating with cubs or other pride members while hunting or patrolling their territory.
13.	Elephants have 4,000 muscles in their trunk.	**False** An Elephant's trunk contains over 40,000 muscles! BONUS: An Elephant calf will often suck their trunk for comfort—just as human babies suck their thumbs.
14.	A Giraffe's tongue is dark blue/purple.	**True** Giraffe's extremely tough tongues have a very high melanin content that gives their tongues a blue/purple hue. Their tongue can be up to 20 inches long!
15.	Adult Lions typically feed every 2-4 days.	**True** Lions need, on average, between 10 and 15 pounds of meat a day, yet do not eat daily. They can go more than a week without feeding and can eat up to 100 pounds of meat at a time.
16.	Elephant sweat glands are located under their ears.	**False** Elephants have very few sweat glands on their body, and those they have are located between their toes.
17.	Impala are called the Bush MacDonalds because of their impressive high numbers.	**False** The Impala gets this name from the black stripes on their rumps, which resemble the golden arches of the fast-food chain.

18.	The Baobab Tree is also known as the tree of life.	**True** The Baobab Tree gets this name because of its water-storage capabilities, edible fruit, various medicinal qualities and uses, and its longevity of thousands of years.
19.	The Bush people of the Kalahari Desert are called the Maasai.	**False** The San people are the oldest indigenous hunter-gatherers of the Kalahari Desert. Like many other indigenous people, they have faced poverty, discrimination, and land theft.
20.	Bushbucks are among the smallest Antelopes found throughout Africa.	**True** Bushbucks, typically only two to three feet tall at the shoulder, are shy, elusive, and great jumpers that can jump at least twice their height.
21.	The Marabou Stork is the only bird to have 2 toes.	**False** The Ostrich is the only bird with two toes.
22.	A Leopard's spots are called rosettes.	**True** A Leopard's black, tan, and yellow markings are unique to each Leopard and are used as camouflage. The rosettes are square in Southern African Leopards and round in Eastern African Leopards.

23.	A Cheetah's toe claws are not retractable.	**True** Unlike those of other Cats, they are only mildly curved and quite blunt.
24.	A Hyena's "laugh" travels further than a Lion's roar.	**False** While their laugh can travel up to three miles, a Lion's roar can travel up to five miles.
25.	On average, a male Lion hunts for 7-9 hours per day.	**False** On average, male Lions sleep 16—20 hours a day

Good Night

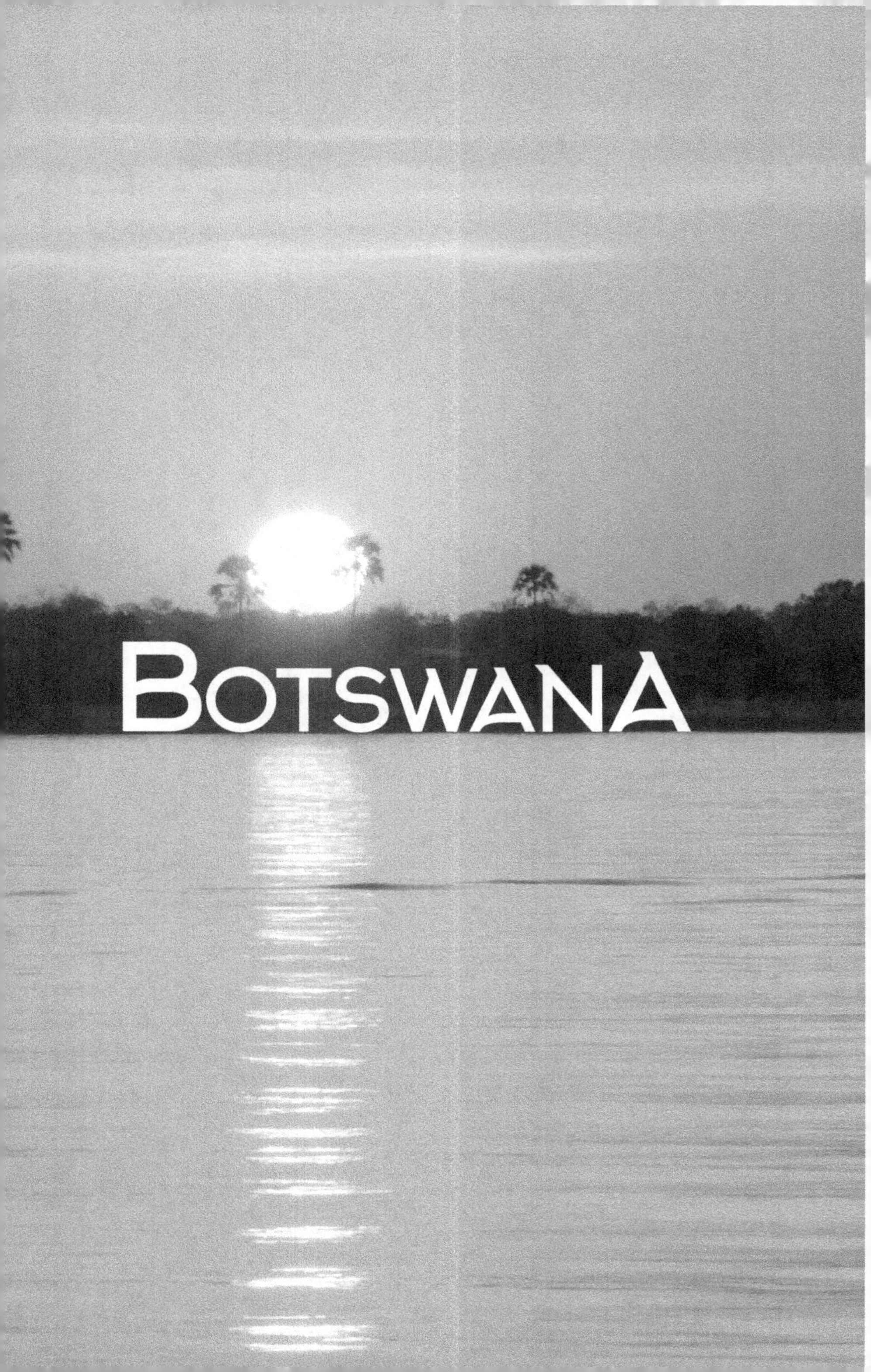
BOTSWANA